Dedicated to men and women who bravely answered the nation's call despite fears and uncertainty; Courageously accepting a life of unknown challenges in the pursuit of something bigger than themselves. To those selflessly dedicated to preservation of freedom. You represent less than 1% of America, but you are the best part because you are my family.

Kevin W. Porter

JOINING THE U.S. MILITARY

Everything You Need To Know

Your Recruiter Won't Tell You

Kevin W. Porter

Kevin W. Porter

TABLE OF CONTENTS

Kevin W. Porter

PREFACE

Several years ago I recognized a problem with our military's recruiting efforts and the lack of transparency being conveyed to our youth. As a recruiter for the Army myself, I saw each branch of the military functioning more like competing businesses in their recruiting efforts. Each branch would act as though they offered the best opportunity meanwhile down-playing their rivaling sister services in an attempt to gain more recruits. I felt this did a certain injustice to those who were considering service to their country because it did not put focus on what was in the best interest of that individual.

Recruiters hold a significant amount of power and control in their hands whether they realize it or not. They have the ability to sway the careers and lives of people just by the amount of information they do or do not offer. I'm writing this book to empower you with the knowledge and level the playing field with your recruiter.

When I was at the point in my life of considering military service, I didn't know anything but I had myself convinced that I knew everything. It's dangerous being in that state of mind while making life decisions on your own, and relying on the guidance of a biased recruiter. Looking back I realize that I was not prepared to ask the right questions and make an informed decision. I had tunnel vision on getting a specific job but no real understanding of the real world or what I needed for my life. Every day I speak with people who are in the same position I was in, and yet they have no clue what life has in store for them.

Many people seem to lack direction in life and are only "winging it" day-by-day. They work with little or no plan towards vague goals in hopes they will obtain success. That's a terrible plan for life and will only keep you trapped in your situation.

My goal with this book is not to tell you what you should be doing with your life or trying to motivate you to get on course with your purpose. There are plenty of books out there for self-discovery. I wrote this book for the men and women who have the military in their sights and want to serve their country. I chose this topic in an effort to look after the future service members of our great nation to ensure they are given the proper guidance and direction for their military careers.

The military has a phenomenal leadership development program designed with mentoring Soldiers to maximize on their careers and accept roles of greater responsibility. However, that level of care and attention in development doesn't always extend beyond the ranks to the individuals who are considering serving. This book will provide you with the right knowledge to make better decisions about your military career. It is my hope that by understanding what is possible for your future, you can have a better discussion with your recruiter and make a solid plan for your career with the U.S. military.

Kevin W. Porter

INTRODUCTION

So you're thinking about joining the world's greatest military? I congratulate you for giving it consideration. It's not an easy decision to put your life on hold to pursue a career in the Armed Forces. Many Americans hesitate to take that leap of faith for various reasons. Most fail to understand what serving in the military truly entails, like the sacrifices made and the dangers faced. This book is designed to help you understand the military misconceptions while educating you on the key benefits of serving. It is not only your guide through the process of planning your military career, but also a tool to determine which branch will be most advantageous for you while helping you determine what questions to ask your recruiter that will maximize your opportunities.

Now with that being said, it's important to understand that not everyone can or even should serve in the military. Most of those who'll want to serve may not even qualify for enlistment for any number of reasons. Some reasons could include certain medical limitations like asthma or depression. Legal trouble such as criminal charges could also prevent you from enlistment. Lacking a high school diploma may hinder your ability to qualify but exceptions have been made from time-to-time depending on the education received after high school.

Enlistment qualification policies change periodically in order to reduce or expand the military force. This is so the Department of Defense can focus on having a military that is not only highly qualified, but also deadly effective. So don't assume you're qualified or disqualified until you've had a talk with your recruiter. They may be able to guide you to becoming qualified if possible. We'll cover this in more detail in a later chapter.

Why should you even listen to what I have to say? For 5 years I served as an Army Recruiter, working for the New York City Recruiting Battalion. I recruited in Suffolk County, Long Island. During my recruiter career, I talked with many individuals who knew absolutely nothing about the military lifestyle. Even worse, what they did "know" was mostly based on what they had seen in Hollywood movies. Some had family that served during the draft days like Vietnam. That made having a conversation very challenging because they immediately assumed that by talking with a recruiter, we're going to scoop them up and send them off to war. As absurd as that may sound, it's a reality that most recruiters face on a daily basis.

Even though I've served and recruited for the U.S. Army, and thoroughly enjoyed my experiences as a Soldier, this book is not about promoting the Army. Every person has a path to follow for the sake of their dreams, and each branch of service has something unique to offer that will help you achieve that dream.

Before you decide to embark on one of the most patriotic acts you will ever experience in your life, it's crucially important to educate yourself about the aspects of serving. I want to help you compare each branch of the military, and show you how your choices will play an impact on your career so you can make an informed decision. So let's get started.

Kevin W. Porter

WHY SHOULD YOU

SERVE?

Why do you want to join the military? This question is usually the starting point for most recruiters. Trying to understand your frame of mind and what brought you into the recruiter's office helps them steer you into a path that will not only be mutually beneficial, but gives them the ammunition to close the deal.

What are you trying to accomplish? Who do you want to be? How do you want people to see you? What do you want from this one life you've been given? How do you want to be remembered? These are the most important questions that you have to ask yourself. Take a moment to really think about these questions and where you see yourself in 3–5 years. The answers to these questions are driving you in life, maybe directly or indirectly. However, it's quite possible that you're just living life day-to-day without purpose or direction; that was my story.

I made the decision to serve my country when I was 20 years old. Until that point, I hadn't figured out my life. I grew up in a low-income household in the country-side of Lexington, NC.

I graduated high school in 2005 in the bottom 20% of my class. I had no plan for college or my career. I was too busy skateboarding and hanging out with my friends to think about my future. At the time I wanted to be a professional skateboarder, but was far from actualizing that dream. When I graduated school, I moved out of my parent's home and in with my aunt and uncle, who, at the time, were my employers as well. Both were well-established entrepreneurs, parents, active community members, and mentors. They both had served in the Army at the beginning of their careers which helped set them up for a more disciplined and ambitious life.

They took me in and tried to provide guidance in my life while I was still lost in my own little world. They gave me an ultimatum from the start; One year to get into college, military, or move out. At 18 years old, I was very stubborn. I was content with working a 9–5 job, skateboarding in my free time, and staying close to friends and family. I heard the phrase many times "get out of this town and go do something with your life. Your friends aren't going anywhere. Most of them will still be working the same dead-end job in a few years and what will you have done during that time?" It took a while for me to realize the life I was living was not the life I wanted for myself, and continuing that path would lead me to an undesirable future if I didn't make sacrifices. I could have gone to college using financial aid or student debt but I had just spent 12 years of my life in school, bored out of my mind. It felt like I was just cramming study material to regurgitate it on test day and brain dump it the next. Many classes in high school were on subjects that most students have to question, "Am I really going to use this in life?" For me, so far the answer has been no.

Fast forward through two years of stagnation. I had to move out because I didn't get my life on track. I spent the next two years living paycheck to paycheck. I was driving a P.O.S. car I didn't like, to a dead-end job I hated, during which time I was crashing couches when I wasn't sleeping in my car behind abandoned buildings. Life wasn't getting any easier, and I wasn't making smarter decisions. I got a dose of reality and it was a swift kick in my face. As the events in my life continued to turn for worse, I was given a second chance to get my life together. My aunt and uncle asked me to move back in with them, under the same ultimatum. I had one year to get into college or the military or I was on my own again. I took it much more serious this time because I knew what was at stake.

I started college in the spring semester of 2007. At this point, I still had no idea what I was doing with my life or what career I was pursuing. I was just trying to keep a roof over my head and make some progress going forward but it all felt like a show. Two years out of high school and I still felt disinterested with classroom education, being lectured to by a teacher who most likely had no real-world experience with the subjects they were teaching. So about one month into college I dropped out of my classes. At this point, I started seriously considering my military options. My aunt and uncle had discussed the benefits of serving many times. In addition to that, a friend of mine had just enlisted into the Coast Guard and was trying to persuade me to take the leap as well. So I started reaching out to recruiters.

Now, because of my hesitations to join the military, I took my time with the process. I started talking with the Coast Guard and eventually took the Armed Services Vocational Aptitude Battery test (ASVAB) only to be disappointed with my job options. I had hoped I could land a job working as a cameraman because it was something I was passionate about from my time creating skateboarding videos. What I didn't know at the time was that due to the Coast Guard being such a small military service, their job options were greatly limited. I then spoke with each of the other branches before finally deciding to go with the Air Force. I didn't exactly make the most educated decision when it came to selecting the Air Force as my final choice. I came to that decision because too many people had said: "it's the safest branch." As I said, I put no thought into that decision or where it would lead me. I had no regard for career opportunities, special skill schools, promotion rates, etc. When you're young and dumb, you don't know what you don't know.

I took the leap, enlisted with the Air Force and was put on a year-long waiting list to ship to boot camp. They allowed me to make a "wish list" of jobs I wanted based on my qualifications, and their plan was to ship me to training whenever the first of those jobs was available. There was no guarantee that I would receive the top job I wanted. All in all, I was just happy to be moving into a new chapter of my life. It was exciting, and I was proud to let everyone know I was finally joining.

Six months later I was growing impatient. I continued to pester my recruiter for an earlier ship date but nothing came of it. It was at that point I decided to see if better opportunities were available with the Army and as luck would have it, there were.

I had the hard talk with my Air Force recruiter to let him know that I was terminating my contract to enlist with the Army. A few weeks later I found myself on a bus heading to Fort Jackson, South Carolina for Basic Combat Training. Looking back, this ended up being a much better decision for me for a multitude of reasons that I won't go into for this story because it sets biased precedence on the Army and this book is not about promoting the Army; this book is about helping you make the right decision for you.

I share my story with you because, like you, I also made the decision to serve. I knew that it was going to better my life, but I had to accept that there would be some sacrifices on my part in order to get where I needed to go. I pursued this opportunity with very little guidance. I took the leap of faith because I needed it. I needed it like I needed air to breathe. It was no one else's responsibility to take care of me, and it would have been childish for me to behave in a manner that suggested otherwise.

I hit hard times early in life and it was that experience that gave me the jolt to wake up, get my head on straight, and be intentional about my goals. It was serving that gave me the discipline to do what was necessary for the sake of my future.

So ask yourself again, why? Why join the military when you can go to college? Why join the military when you can get a job in your hometown close to your friends and family? Why join the military when you can sleep safely and comfortably in your bed every night? I'm not asking you these questions to talk you out of the decision to serve. I'm asking you these questions because they will define you. They will help you find the confidence in yourself to make that tough decision.

Find your reason and you will find your commitment to serve. Recruiters will tell you all the great benefits there are for serving. They'll tell you about all the cool stuff you'll do and places you could go. That's great, but those are the benefits of serving, not the reason for serving. Trust me, if you join the military for one of the benefits, you'll find yourself miserable every day until you get out of the service. The reason I say this is because serving in the military is not exactly easy. There will be days that suck. There will be people who push your buttons and test your patience. There will be moments when you're pushed to your mental and physical limits and you just want to throw in the towel and call it quits. But will you? Or will the reason you're there in the first place be strong enough to keep your head in the game? Once you've found your reason, read on.

THE PERCEPTION &

THE TRUTH

As a kid, if you've ever played war games or watched action movies of brave men on the battlefield, it's likely left you inspired with a shot of adrenaline and motivation. You've probably thought that you could see yourself out on the front-lines, living a life filled with adventure and heroism. But now you're an adult and you have to more carefully weigh your career decisions.

The idea of action that once got your heart racing may no longer seem like a viable career path. Many parents are acutely aware of this, and are often most terrified at the thought of their children joining the military for good reason. But it's often on a complete misunderstanding that many have of the military.

Misperception #1

Everyone who joins the military will be on the "front lines."

I believe this misperception was built in Hollywood because every time a movie depicts Soldiers deploying, they always build the story around war and the battlefield.

When a person joins the military, they do so with the intent to learn a skill. This skill is what the Department of Defense is paying them to do for their branch of the military. While stateside, their responsibility is to increase their skill-set through training so that they may be a valuable asset to a team if and when they deploy overseas. What this skill entails is completely dependent upon the branch they serve in. What I mean by this is that each branch offers different types of careers based on their needs and mission responsibilities. So if you're an infantryman in the Marine Corps, your job is to learn small team fighting tactics and perfect the art so that you're more effective in a combat environment. If you are a cook in the Navy, your job is to learn how to prepare meals that are both delicious and nutritious so if you're out at sea for months at a time, your unit can be properly fed and capable of completing their mission. If you're an intelligence analyst for the Army, your job is to effectively understand intelligence and prepare it so that it can be comprehensible by those who will be using it for mission planning. Long story short, the job you're trained to do is the skillset you're expected to perform if you're ever deployed.

Now with that being said, there is one key point that you must know. Everyone who serves must complete Basic (Combat) Training or "Boot Camp." This training is designed to help you develop into a fighter and operate with a team. Not because you will fight, but because you need to always be prepared for when a situation calls for action. Let me give you a scenario. You're currently deployed with your unit in the Middle East. Your job as a mechanic is to repair or replace HUMVEEs that have been damaged during convoy operations. Suddenly enemy fire breaks out along the perimeter and the perimeter guards are outnumbered. If terrorists are lucky enough to get past the guards, then every Soldier needs to know how to operate their weapon and defend their base. That is, of course, a worst-case scenario. The reality is that anything is possible and it's best that everyone knows what to do when the situation presents itself. You'll find that your training will quickly kick-in and your responses will be more instinctual.

Misperception #2

Everyday life in the military is like Basic Training.

If you're envisioning military life like Stanley Kubrick's film "Full Metal Jacket" with Ronald Lee Ermey in your face, wearing you down day after day until there is no soul left in you, then you and I were on the same page. Fortunately that isn't the case.

Basic training can be physically and mentally challenging for anyone, but that is only to break you off from who you were and build you into who you need to be. The military training environment is designed to induce stress so that as you develop, you're capable of thinking and performing in less than ideal conditions. Once you leave the training environment and are assigned to your first base, your daily lifestyle is not much different from your civilian life. Here is an example of a typical day from my experience.

6:30 am	Meet with your unit for Physical Training (PT)
7:30 am	Go home for a shower, breakfast, and get ready for work
9:00 am	Report to the office for work or training
11:30 am	Lunch break
1:00 pm	Return to work
5:00 pm	Close-out

Please keep in mind that I am leaving out a significant number of details for the sake of a simple understanding that the work schedule is very similar to your typical 9-5. This schedule can and will vary depending on your job and how your unit needs to modify the schedule to meet their mission requirements. For instance, if you're working as Military Police, you may get the night shift for a few weeks. In this case, the time may be different but the structure should be the same. This also doesn't take into account the various training activities that could be happening on a particular day. For example, instead of working at your office, one day you may be at the range qualifying with your weapon. On another day, you may be in the field practicing your land navigation skills with your platoon. The activity may change and the time frame can alter depending on mission requirements, but those are unique events. I would not consider these events to be a day to day norm. However, it does depend on your unit's mission and need for training.

Misperception #3

Joining the military will put me behind in my college education.

Perhaps there is some truth to this. I won't try to sugarcoat the fact that, yes, while you serve in the military you may not complete your college degree at the same speed as someone who goes directly to college. However, let's consider the facts. You can enroll into college straight out of high school using financial aid and student loans. At that time, you probably have no marketable skills that allow you to get a job for much more than minimum wage, and because you're going to school full-time, you're working less than the number of hours you really need to make a livable wage. So you make a pathetic paycheck each week that helps you with gas and food. That low income also forces you to live at home with your parents. Maybe you're fortunate enough to get a decent scholarship that carries you most, if not all the way through college. For the majority of the student population that isn't the case.

So think about where all this leaves you. You finish college already tens of thousands of dollars in debt. You're around 23 years old and still living with your parents. Now you're entering the workforce, looking for a job of which statistics have been showing for years is becoming increasingly harder for college graduates to find work in the field they've been studying. So you take another dead-end job in the mean-time. I bet that sounds like someone you know.

Consider this military advantage.

You may not be able to go to college full-time while serving full-time, but for the part-time college you are obtaining, the military is paying for it so you get a debt-free degree.

You not only get a classroom education from the military but also real-world experience. That, combined with your degree, makes you tremendously marketable to future employers and highly competitive to your civilian counterparts.

Additionally, your military training is recorded on your Joint Service Transcript. This is comparable to a college transcript for what you have learned during your service. Colleges also grant credits for much of the training you've received during the service, which allows you to finish your degree faster, by skipping those classes.

Many service members also receive secret and top-secret clearances from the military that help them land better career opportunities at higher salaries when they are leaving the service and joining the civilian workforce.

You're getting paid while you serve, so therefore, you're getting paid while going to college. Oh, and you're NOT living with your parents. What's not to love?

Listen, I could go on and on with this. Ask any service member out there and they'll tell you. They're far better off having served in the military and worked towards their degree on the side. It's a no-brainer. If you're worried that your time in the military is going to slow you from getting that dream job, have you considered that your dream job may be offered in the military?

Misperception #4

The pay and benefits are not enough to make a decent living.

I've heard this statement on many occasions. "Soldiers don't get paid enough." What this suggests is, for the sacrifices they make, service members should be getting paid significantly higher. Of course, we all want to get paid more. Some men and women have made the ultimate sacrifice, and others come face-to-face with that reality every time they deploy to a war zone. That threat definitely warrants an unfathomable salary. However, this notion that troops are not well paid may be misunderstood to the ill-informed. Take this example into consideration.

	Civilian Job Police Patrol Officer	Army Job Military Police Sergeant	Civilian Job Police Patrol Officer	Army Job Military Police Sergeant
Family	Single	Single	Family of four	Family of four
Rank/Years of service	N/A	E5 4 yrs	N/A	E5 4 yrs
Salary	$53,867	$33,652	$53,867	$33,652
Housing	$0	$14,688	$0	$16,920
Food Allowance	$0	$4,433	$0	$4,433
Tax Advantages	$0	$2,607	$0	$2,372
Health Care	$9,858	Included	$22,819	Included
NET INCOME	$44,009	$53,380	$31,048	$57,377

https://www.goarmy.com/benefits/total-compensation.html

This chart breaks down total compensation in a comparison between two similar professions: a civilian police officer and a military police Sergeant. To those who quickly try to compare salary to salary, they would easily recognize that the civilian officer wins. However, when you dig deeper into the financial compensation, you'll see that the Soldier receives more monetary benefits. This chart doesn't even include the additional income that can be made for acquiring special skills such as parachutist and diving.

As you can see, serving in the military can actually be more financially beneficial. This chart only skims the surface of what benefits are received through the military. For instance, serving for three years on active duty will qualify you with a significant scholarship towards your college education in addition to the tuition assistance that you receive while you serve.

What most people fail to realize is that while serving, a large portion of military income is tax-free. That means more money goes into your pocket rather than to the IRS. It's also important to note that even though this example was taken from the U.S. Army website, pay and allowances are not branch specific. What I mean is that you do not make more money for being in one branch over another. Pay and benefits are dictated from the Department of Defense so there is financial equality among the military. What will make a difference in your income, however, is how fast you get promoted in one branch or the other. I will cover this in more detail in a later chapter.

What are some negative comments you've heard about serving in the military? I challenge you to seek out people who have served and pick their brain. I would also recommend that you talk with those who have served more recently, perhaps within the last decade. The reason I say this is because times have changed. The hardships that troops faced during the Vietnam era are not likely to be hardships affecting troops in the 21st century. As we continue to evolve as a society, life gets better, including military life. Just keep that in mind as you do your own research.

ACTIVE DUTY,

RESERVE, &

NATIONAL GUARD

If you've made the decision to serve your country, now you have to decide how much time you intend to commit to your future military career. Yes, you have choices! I know some people think that joining the military is a full-time job and there is no other way about it but that's not the case. This chapter will help you understand the options you have, and how they will increase or restrict your opportunities going forward.

Active Duty

These are your full-timers. The men and women that put on the uniform day-in and day-out for years of their lives. These heroes agree to leave their family, friends, homes, and lives behind to start a new career with the military in order to serve and protect their country. Active-duty troops invest years at a time to the service of our nation as they serve their respective branches throughout the world. They make up the majority of the U.S. military force. The active-duty component of the military works for the Department of Defense (federally funded).

Why choose active duty? Well, if you're like me and need a way to get out on your own, want to travel the world, yet still support yourself financially then active duty has you covered. Working on active duty comes with the greatest amount of compensation for any of the components mentioned in this chapter, but it also comes with the greatest amount of sacrifices.

First off, you receive training in a job with no previous experience necessary (and you get paid while you're training). Then, you get to live in a new and exciting location. Depending on what branch you ultimately decide will play a big role in where you get stationed. You will be provided food and housing free of charge. Once you get settled into your new home, you will be able to attend college paid for by the government. You will have access to many resources and benefits over the course of your service and to go into them all I would need to write another book!

If you're young and have no obligations in your life at the moment, going active is by far the best route to go. Active duty will help you get your head on straight, get your life on track, and give you the resources to ignite your career.

Reserve

These are your "weekend warriors." The guys and gals who serve one weekend a month in addition to two full weeks every year. They are the nation's supporting military force.

This component of the armed forces works part-time within their hometowns, training and preparing for the moment that their unit may be called to action. The reserve component of the military also works for the Department of Defense (federally funded).

Reserve troops invest a very small fraction of their lives in their service. In doing so, they are compensated at a rate smaller than that of active duty Soldiers. They do not receive full medical coverage for free like their active counterparts.

Instead, reservists receive medical benefits at a steep discount than that of any civilian. Reservists will receive college benefits, but not to the same extent that the active-duty component will receive. They usually have to rely on additional resources like financial aid, grants, or student loans to help bridge the financial gap of tuition expenses. Luckily, there are resources like the Yellow Ribbon Program designed to assist service members, both past and present, with any extensive tuition costs. Colleges participating will match dollar for dollar up to a designated amount in order to assist those service members with attending their college.

One distinct advantage that is beneficial to serving in the Reserve is the quick skill training that you receive. If you choose to serve on reserve status you will, at some point, leave for basic training and your job training. Once you have completed your training, you'll return home to pick up life where you left off, but now you'll be equipped with additional skills that can help you become more marketable in the workforce. Depending on the training you receive may determine what new job opportunities you have available and what your starting income may be. In addition to these new skills, the military may have provided you with a security clearance that can be very valuable in the civilian sector. Because of these considerations, it makes the possibilities nearly endless for anyone coming straight out of high school to be successful.

Why choose the Reserve? Those who serve in the Reserve do so for many reasons. Some of the most common reasons are so that they may be able to pursue or continue college at a full-time pace; using their military service benefits to help supplement their college tuition. Others may serve on reserve status because they have a great career at home and want to see it through. There are also those who serve in the Reserve because they want to do their part for the country but don't want to leave home. Either way, reserve duty can be a very viable option to supplement your current income, career goals, or college studies.

National Guard

Much like the Reserve, the National Guard is a part-time commitment to the service you choose. What separates the National Guard from its two counterparts is that the National Guard is managed by the Department of Homeland

Security and is funded by their respective states. For instance, if you're working for the Army National Guard of New York, then New York state funds your unit, not the federal government. The purpose of the National Guard is to protect each individual state from various threats such as natural disasters, domestic terrorism, or even overreach of power from the federal government.

Currently, there are only two services that offer opportunities for the National Guard. That is the Army National Guard and the Air National Guard. The Army National Guard is the original U.S. military force and is the only branch of the military that is actually a constitutional requirement. The Air National Guard is a subordinate component of the Air Force and serves with the same state-bound distinction as the Army National Guard.

How to decide which is right for you

Deciding which component to go with might be a very simple answer once you have decided what you want for your life. The next question you have to ask yourself is how do you get there? Each component has its pros and cons. It's up to you to decide which of these options will provide you with the most resources to help you get to your destination.

The active option may provide you with more income and stability while you attend college on the side, but it may take you twice as long to complete your college education. The Reserve option may give you more time to complete your college education and build your civilian career, but not provide you with enough financial support to make ends meet. The National Guard option may give you location stability while you focus on college, but possibly restrict you from going into active duty in the future.

In my experience, this decision is often the most challenging for people. Joining the military is a leap of faith with a contractual obligation, causing most people to base their decision on the least commitment necessary. That is not always the best decision considering each person's circumstances and goals. I encourage you to write out your 3-5 year goals and prioritize them from most to least important. After you have done this, you will find some clarity with what you need to accomplish. This will help you and your recruiter decide which of these options makes the most sense for your future.

Keep in mind as you're deciding which path to take, that your plans may change a year or two down the road. That doesn't mean that your military career cannot change with it. Many service members leave active duty at the end of their contract to switch to the Reserve. Just the same, some Reserve members switch to active duty when they see the need for a full-time career with the military. Be sure to have this conversation with your recruiter about your ability to switch components as your life changes.

If you're unsure about your decision or the feedback you're receiving from your recruiter, talk with another recruiter, speak with someone you may know who has some military experience, or find an online forum where people are sharing their experiences openly so you can confirm what you need to know.

YOUR CONTRACT IS NOT LIKE THE OTHERS

Everyone who agrees to join the military has to sign a contract. However, not everyone receives the same contract. Of course, each contract is different because each person joining the military is making different commitments. Some will agree to serve for 2 years all the way up to 6 years. One key detail that is usually left unmentioned by recruiters, can make or break your military career if left unnoticed. I'm talking about the difference between open contracts and closed contracts.

Before I dig into the specifics of what separates the two, I want to explain to you the general essence of the military contract.

The Military Contract

The military contact, also known as the DD Form 4, is the standard document for anyone who is enlisting into any branch of the Armed Forces. This document consists of 4 pages. The first page is the most significant because it establishes the "agreements" between you and your future employer. This form will outline the specific details that have been promised to you for serving your country.

The first section of the contract (known as Block A) is primarily your identification data. Typical personal information consisting of your name, date of birth, social security number, date of enlistment, etc. Block B, however, is where you need to pay closer attention because this is your agreements section. This section starts off by identifying which branch of the military you will be serving with. It then states the number of years of your commitment, and whether it's active duty or Reserve. The following section will specify what pay grade you will enter the service as. We'll talk about pay grades more in the next chapter but for now, you need to understand that this pay grade is identifying your rank. The subsequent gaps in the form identify how your time will be served. As you continue to read on you'll notice "I must serve a total of (8) years." This is called the Minimum Service Obligation.

Minimum Service Obligation

If your recruiter was thorough in providing you with all the facts, they should not have left this significant detail out. The Minimum Service Obligation or MSO for short is an established standard "backup plan" for all branches of the military. To understand how it works, let's say you join the Navy for 3 years of Active duty. During those 3 years, you will be employed by the Navy. However, when those 3 years of active duty are over, you still have 5 years remaining on your contract in order to complete your 8-year MSO. Once you leave the Navy, you are now in the Inactive Ready Reserve aka IRR. While in the IRR, you are living your life on your terms. You are back to being a civilian again, but with one stipulation.

The IRR was designed as the military "backup plan" for the government. If tensions escalate between the U.S. and its enemies, there may be a need to prepare for war very quickly. If there is no time to train new troops to fill positions necessary for the war, the U.S. may seek to recall those who are in the IRR because they are already trained and experienced in a needed skillset.

If you serve in the military for 8 or more years, you will not have an MSO to fulfill any longer because you served the full 8-year requirement. So when you depart the military, you are not at risk for being called back to action. If you serve for less than 8 years, you will find yourself in the IRR until your MSO is complete. Don't worry though, the chances of the military calling you back to action are pretty slim. The Department of Defense does a great job of planning ahead and incentivizing enlistments to keep our armed forces an all-volunteer service.

Delayed Entry/Enlistment Program

In the next section of the contract, you'll find the delayed entry/enlistment program. This program is what all new recruits find themselves in once they enlist. After you've signed your contract, you will be working with your recruiter to prepare for basic training. In most cases, this will include physical fitness training and studying to understand the military culture and rank structure. It is nothing more than spending a few hours a week with your recruiter. This allows the recruiter to keep you excited and energetic about your decision to serve while training you to be more effective once you ship out for basic training.

Remarks

The remarks section happens to be one of the most valuable sections of your contract. This is where any promises or agreements are put into writing. This section will identify the specifics of your contact from what job you will be trained into and any bonuses that you're entitled to. Pay very close attention to this area of your contract. It's worth mentioning because what you may not know about military contracts may shock you. Not every branch offers the same type of contract.

Open Contract

The term "open contract" is recruiter lingo so you won't find any details about it on any of the different military websites. An open contract has different names to each branch of the military that offer it. What you need to understand is the general idea behind what an open contract is so you can spot when it is being offered to you.

An open contract, in its simplistic form, is an agreement from you to enlist with a branch of the military, but no specific job has been promised to you. You're joining the military but have no plan for your career. When you sign this contract, you are essentially saying "I am willing to do whatever job is given to me." Some people may find this to be of no concern because they just want to serve. Others may have serious problems with this because they have very specific career goals and do not want to find themselves doing something less desirable.

To some of the smaller branches of the military, this gives flexibility for shipping recruits. At the same time, it's the smaller branches that take the longest to ship their recruits to training due to limited training availability.

Closed Contract

As you can imagine, a closed contract would be just the opposite. It's an agreement from you to serve in the military but the branch has guaranteed you a specific job. With a closed contract, you know upfront what terms you're agreeing to so nothing catches you off guard. This is so crucially important for you to understand because you may have a long term career path planned out, and serving in the military with a specific job helps you get the training you need to start in the right direction. This also increases your chances of fast-tracking through college by using your military training from your Joint Service Transcript for college credits. We'll cover this more in chapter 10. A closed contract gives you the control to ensure that you're getting exactly what you agreed to.

There is a caveat to that last paragraph that I want to make perfectly clear. Yes, with a closed contract you will be able to lock in a specific job and it's incentives. However, in order for you to keep that job for your career, you must complete the training requirements. It should go without saying that if you cannot complete the job training that the military has given you, maybe you're not cut-out to work in that particular job. In those circumstances, you may find yourself being switched to a different job that is more appropriate to your qualifications. More often than not, the branch that you're serving in will offer to retrain you with the subject that you're struggling with. However, if you're not grasping the course material after one or two retests, it's time to stop wasting tax payer's dollars and train you in something you can wrap your head around.

What Each Branch Offers

If you speak with any recruiter of any branch, you're sure to find that they all offer "guaranteed jobs." I say it like that because they all want to have the best opportunities to offer over any other branch. Especially if it means that whoever is asking will join their branch. The reality is much different. Yes, all branches do offer guaranteed jobs but most offer undesignated jobs which is most common. What I mean by undesignated is that you are not assigned a specific job. Instead, you are assigned to a general career path. For instance, if you scored very well in the electronics section of the ASVAB, your branch would assign you to that field. You would later discover what job within that field you would be working in. The Army is the only branch that offers strictly guaranteed jobs due to the vast amount of jobs available and frequent shipping dates. Each of the other branches offer a combination of guaranteed jobs and undesignated jobs.

While it may not be such a bad thing to contract for an undesignated job, it is far from ideal if you have a long term career plan established.

Keep the following in mind: most people that are joining the military have no experience or qualifications for the job they're requesting. While it is my personal recommendation that you chase a job that is in line with your career goals, understand that beggars cannot be choosers. Your recruiter is doing favors and working miracles to help you join. Don't demand a job for which you do not qualify or deserve. You would not go to a job interview and demand that the company hire you to be a heart surgeon when all you have is a high school diploma and job experience at McDonald's. The same applies when joining the military. Be reasonable.

PAY &

ENTITLEMENTS

Who doesn't love money? I can hear some critics out there saying "money isn't everything" and of course, it isn't. We both know that you're not planning to serve your country for free so you want to make your time worth the service. As I mentioned before, salary and benefits are universal across all branches of the military. So when you're considering which branch to serve, don't allow income to play a role in your decision.

If you're active duty, your pay will not begin until you arrive at basic training. Yes, this means that you get paid while in training. Most employers won't do that for you. Keep in mind, however, that you won't receive a physical paycheck. Instead, your income will be deposited directly into your bank account on the 1st and 15th of the month if you choose bi-weekly payments, or on the 1st alone if you chose monthly. I have personally found that by using the monthly paycheck option, I am able to manage my finances better and budget more effectively.

If you're serving in the Reserve or National Guard, your pay will begin when you attend drill weekend aka "battle assembly." Because these drill weekends take place once a month, you may attend and receive payment before you've even attended boot camp. For those that are serving in either of these two components, you will receive active duty (full-time) pay when you're at training because you're on an active status. The chart that follows is how base pay (or salary) is broken down for each branch of the military serving on active duty.

MONTHLY BASIC PAY TABLE
EFFECTIVE 1 JANUARY 2019
YEARS OF SERVICE

PAY GRADE	<2	2	3	4	6	8	10	12	14	16	18	20	22	24	26	28	30	32	34	36	38	40
									COMMISSIONED OFFICERS													
O-10	0.00	0.00	0.00	0.00	0.00	0.00	0.00	0.00	0.00	0.00	0.00	16025.10	16025.10	16025.10	16025.10	16025.10	16025.10	16025.10	16025.10	16025.10	16025.10	16025.10
O-9	0.00	0.00	0.00	0.00	0.00	0.00	0.00	0.00	0.00	0.00	0.00	15078.60	15296.40	15610.20	16025.10	16025.10	16025.10	16025.10	16025.10	16025.10	16025.10	16025.10
O-8	10868.90	11018.70	11250.60	11315.40	11604.90	12088.20	12200.70	12653.70	12791.70	13187.10	13759.50	14287.20	14639.40	14639.40	14639.40	14639.40	15006.60	15006.00	15380.70	15380.70	15380.70	15380.70
O-7	8865.30	9276.00	9467.70	9613.20	9893.40	10164.60	10477.80	10790.10	11103.60	12088.20	12916.20	12919.20	12919.20	12919.20	12985.50	12985.50	13245.30	13245.30	13245.30	13245.30	13245.30	13245.30
O-6	6722.70	7385.70	7870.50	7870.50	7900.50	8230.20	8283.50	8283.90	8754.30	9586.80	10076.20	10563.30	10841.40	11123.10	11668.20	11668.20	11901.30	11901.30	11901.30	11901.30	11901.30	11901.30
O-5	5604.30	6313.50	6750.00	6832.50	7105.50	7268.10	7627.20	7890.90	8230.80	8751.30	8998.50	9243.60	9521.40	9521.40	9521.40	9521.40	9521.40	9521.40	9521.40	9521.40	9521.40	9521.40
O-4	4835.40	5597.40	5971.20	6054.00	6400.80	6772.80	7236.00	7595.30	7846.50	7990.50	8073.90	8073.90	8073.90	8073.90	8073.90	8073.90	8073.90	8073.90	8073.90	8073.90	8073.90	8073.90
O-3	4251.60	4819.20	5201.40	5671.50	5943.60	6241.50	6434.40	6751.20	6916.80	6916.80	6916.80	6916.80	6916.80	6916.80	6916.80	6916.80	6916.80	6916.80	6916.80	6916.80	6916.80	6916.80
O-2	3673.50	4183.80	4818.30	4981.20	5083.80	5083.80	5083.80	5083.80	5083.80	5083.80	5083.80	5083.80	5083.80	5083.80	5083.80	5083.80	5083.80	5083.80	5083.80	5083.80	5083.90	5083.90
O-1	3188.40	3318.80	4011.90	4011.90	4011.90	4011.90	4011.90	4011.90	4011.90	4011.90	4011.90	4011.90	4011.90	4011.90	4011.90	4011.90	4011.90	4011.90	4011.90	4011.90	4011.90	4011.90
									COMMISSIONED OFFICERS WITH OVER 4 YEARS ACTIVE DUTY SERVICE													
								AS AN ENLISTED MEMBER OR WARRANT OFFICER														
O-3E	0.00	0.00	0.00	5671.50	5943.60	6241.50	6434.40	6751.20	7018.50	7172.70	7361.80	7361.80	7361.80	7361.80	7361.80	7361.80	7361.80	7361.80	7361.80	7361.80	7361.80	7361.80
O-2E	0.00	0.00	0.00	4981.20	5083.80	5245.50	5518.80	5730.00	5887.20	5887.20	5887.20	5887.20	5887.20	5887.20	5887.20	5887.20	5887.20	5887.20	5887.20	5887.20	5887.20	5887.20
O-1E	0.00	0.00	0.00	4011.90	4284.00	4442.40	4604.40	4763.40	4981.20	4981.20	4981.20	4981.20	4981.20	4981.20	4981.20	4981.20	4981.20	4981.20	4981.20	4981.20	4981.20	4981.20
									WARRANT OFFICERS													
W-5	0.00	0.00	0.00	0.00	0.00	0.00	0.00	0.00	0.00	0.00	0.00	7812.60	8208.90	8503.80	8830.50	8830.50	6272.70	9272.70	9735.60	9735.60	10293.40	10293.4
W-4	4393.80	4726.20	4861.80	4995.30	5225.10	5452.80	5683.20	6029.10	6333.00	6621.90	6858.60	7089.30	7428.00	7706.40	8024.10	8024.10	8184.00	8184.00	8184.00	8184.00	8184.00	8184.00
W-3	4012.50	4179.80	4351.20	4407.90	4589.70	4940.40	5308.50	5482.20	5682.90	5889.00	6261.00	6511.80	6651.80	6821.10	7038.60	7098.80	7098.60	7038.60	7038.80	7038.80	7038.80	7038.80
W-2	3550.50	3888.20	3989.70	4060.80	4290.90	4648.80	4828.10	5000.40	5214.00	5381.10	5532.00	5713.20	5832.00	5926.20	5926.20	5926.20	5926.20	5926.20	5926.20	5926.20	5926.20	5926.20
W-1	3116.40	3452.10	3542.10	3732.60	3957.90	4290.30	4445.10	4992.00	4875.30	5043.30	5197.50	5385.30	5385.30	5385.30	5385.30	5385.30	5385.30	5385.30	5385.30	5385.30	5385.30	5385.30
									ENLISTED MEMBERS													
E-9	0.00	0.00	0.00	0.00	0.00	0.00	5308.20	5428.50	5580.30	5758.20	5938.80	6228.50	6470.70	6725.00	7119.30	7119.30	7474.80	7474.80	7846.90	7846.90	8241.90	8241.90
E-8	0.00	0.00	0.00	0.00	0.00	4345.30	4537.50	4656.80	4796.60	4953.60	5232.30	5373.50	5613.90	5747.40	6075.50	6075.80	6197.70	6197.70	6197.70	6197.70	6197.70	6197.70
E-7	3020.70	3296.70	3423.30	3590.10	3720.90	3945.00	4071.60	4292.70	4482.00	4609.80	4745.40	4757.00	4974.30	5066.80	5429.10	5429.10	5429.10	5429.10	5429.10	5429.10	5429.10	5429.10
E-6	2613.70	2875.20	3002.10	3125.40	3254.10	3643.30	3656.40	3874.50	3941.40	3990.00	4046.70	4046.70	4046.70	4046.70	4046.70	4046.70	4046.70	4046.70	4046.70	4046.70	4046.70	4046.70
E-5	2395.40	2584.80	2678.10	2804.40	3001.50	3207.30	3376.20	3396.60	3396.60	3396.60	3396.60	3396.60	3396.60	3396.60	3396.60	3396.60	3396.60	3396.60	3396.60	3706.70	3396.60	3396.60
E-4	2194.50	2307.00	2431.80	2555.40	2664.00	2664.00	2664.00	2664.00	2664.00	2664.00	2664.00	2664.00	2664.00	2664.00	2664.00	2664.00	2664.00	2664.00	2664.00	2664.00	2664.00	2664.00
E-3	1981.20	2105.70	2233.50	2233.50	2233.50	2233.50	2233.50	2233.50	2233.50	2233.50	2233.50	2233.50	2233.50	2233.50	2233.50	2233.50	2233.50	2233.50	2233.50	2233.50	2233.50	2233.50
E-2	1884.00	1884.00	1884.00	1884.00	1884.00	1884.00	1884.00	1884.00	1884.00	1884.00	1884.00	1884.00	1884.00	1884.00	1884.00	1884.00	1884.00	1884.00	1884.00	1884.00	1884.00	1884.00
E-1 >4 Mon	1680.90	1680.90	1680.90	1680.90	1680.90	1680.90	1680.90	1680.90	1680.90	1680.90	1680.90	1680.90	1680.90	1680.90	1680.90	1680.90	1680.90	1680.90	1680.90	1680.90	1680.90	1680.90
E-1 <4 Mon	1554.00	0.00	0.00	0.00	0.00	0.00	0.00	0.00	0.00	0.00	0.00	0.00	0.00	0.00	0.00	0.00	0.00	0.00	0.00	0.00	0.00	0.00

https://www.dfas.mil/dam/
jcr:a8fe14fa-9234-406b-8b2a-27ab459a6666/MilPayTable2019_3.pdf

From this 2019 pay chart you can see that pay in the military is determined by two factors. The first and most obvious is the rank that you hold (identified in the left column). When initially entering the service, you're starting out at the bottom of the proverbial totem pole. The exception to this rule is if your branch offers early rank advancement for meeting certain qualifications such as having a degree, JROTC, or even valuable job skills. On this chart however, rank is not identified by its name, like Private or

Sergeant. Instead, it is identified by the pay grade associated with the rank.

Not every brand of service identifies its rank the same for it's associated pay grade. For instance, a Staff Sergeant in the Army is an E-6 pay grade, whereas a Staff Sergeant in the Air Force is an E-5.

The second aspect of the pay chart is the years of service. This is important to understand because it implies that you will receive guaranteed pay raises periodically, even if you're not getting promoted. This chart actually extends beyond 20 years, but for the purposes of simplicity, I left it at 20 years. This pay chart shows that you're being incentivized for not only getting promoted but for staying in the service longer.

Lastly, the base pay that we just covered is the only income that you receive that is taxed. The additional income I introduce in this chapter is incentives and allowances, and is non-taxable income.

Annual Pay Raises

Each year, in an effort to keep military wages competitive with civilian wages and to combat inflation, congress authorizes a pay increase for military personnel through the Defense Appropriations Act and the Defense Authorization Act. This usually ranges between 1% and 3%.

Allowances

Housing

Initially starting your military career, you should not expect to receive an allowance for housing. Instead, you should expect to live in military barracks. These are essentially small apartments that you may share with another service member. As you progress and take on a leadership role, you may be afforded allowance to move into your own home or apartment. The timeline for this to take place will depend on your branch and when they deem it reasonable to provide you with a housing allowance. Alternatively, if you're married, you will receive a housing allowance and avoid barracks life. Your housing allowance will be determined by the zip code for your unit, your current pay grade, and whether you have dependents. You can find the housing allowance calculator at http://www.defensetravel.dod.mil/site/bahCalc.cfm

Food

If you find yourself living in the barracks, you will be provided meals free of charge, courtesy of your local dining facility. If you're provided a housing allowance, however, you will also receive allowance for food. This is typically a flat rate that will not vary by location. If your food or living expenses are higher than normal for the location you're in, you may be supplemented with a Cost Of Living Allowance (COLA) to offset the higher prices.

Clothing

Every year on the anniversary of your entry into the military, you will receive a clothing allowance to resupply or replace any uniforms or accessories needed to keep you looking your best. Uniforms can get worn out pretty fast depending on the training or job you may be doing. Most often, you will pay out of your own pocket for the upkeep of your uniforms throughout the year and use the clothing allowance as reimbursement.

Family Separation

As a married service member, you may find yourself away from your family for training or deployments. When this occurs in excess of 30 days, you're provided family separation allowance as compensation for any hardship your lack of presence may have on your family.

Combat

When a service member is deployed to a region of the world that is affected by ongoing combat engagement, they receive combat pay. In addition to the extra allowance, while in a combat zone, they will receive all income at the tax-free rate.

Incentives

Special Skills

With each branch, there are monetary incentives for learning new skills. These skills can vary from branch to branch such as being a parachutist or diver qualified. If you're interested in attending unique schools, do your research to see what your branch offers and the feasibility of being able to attend such schools. I say this because some skill training schools may be harder to attend than others. Your recruiter can help you understand the correct path you need to take to open up these opportunities.

Foreign Language Proficiency Pay

Another way to receive additional incentive pay is to learn a valuable language. When branches of the military have a need to interact with other cultures and language is a barrier, your ability to communicate becomes a valuable asset. Your branch may offer Foreign Language Proficiency Pay if they are able to benefit from your language skills.

Special Duty

Some special positions within the military offer additional income to incentivize troops to take on new roles. This special duty pay is more common in positions such as a Recruiter, Drill Sergeant, or Instructor. Serving in these positions not only fattens your wallet with additional income but demonstrates your capabilities when competing for your next promotion. These special positions are most often reserved specifically for individuals who have already attained leadership roles within their respective branches of service.

Bonuses

Sometimes the military finds themselves needing to recruit positions that are either hard to fill because the job is not desirable, or hard to retain quality troops because the job pays greater in the civilian workforce. When this happens, bonuses are offered to entice service members to take specific opportunities. You may find these bonuses when you're in the process of joining or towards the end of your enlistment term as an incentive for you to reenlist.

Bonuses come and go as military needs are met and positions are filled, so don't expect a bonus when you enlist. Consider it a bonus if you get one. Do you see what I did there? Don't get too caught up in the dollar signs if your recruiter is mentioning bonuses. Keep your eye on the target. You may be chasing a dream job of being an Air Traffic Controller, but they're talking about a 20k bonus for enlisting as a Plumber. Be realistic in your ambitions when considering your qualifications, but remain focused as well. If you know you don't qualify for an Air Traffic Controller position, what's the next best thing that you DO qualify for?

Don't settle for a less than desirable job because it has a nice bonus attached to it. Otherwise, you will find yourself working a job you hate while developing no applicable skills for your future career when you get out of the service.

WHAT MAKES YOUR BRANCH SO SPECIAL

All branches are created equal, right? Wrong! By now, you should have decided on whether active, Reserve or National Guard is right for you. Now you have to decide which branch of the military makes the most sense for your career.

You may be thinking to yourself, as many do, that what really differentiates branches from one another is the types of jobs each may offer and the uniforms they wear. Sure, the Navy has completely different job opportunities than what the Army may have, but that's to be expected because their missions are much different as well. When you dig deeper and look beyond just jobs and uniforms, you'll find that the differences are so vast that it could be the major deciding factor for you.

Promotions

If you like money, promotions are important. If
you like to chase success, promotions are crucial.
If you don't want to be held back from your
potential, promotions are necessary. I can tell you
from first-hand experience, I was not considering
promotions and long-term career opportunities
when I first joined the Army. I was focused on
just taking the first step. It wasn't until I arrived
at my first assignment that I begin chasing
opportunities. I was hungry for responsibilities
and experiences. I knew I had to out-work and
out-think my peers if I wanted to move up in rank
quickly. With that being said, I want you to
understand the end game. Look, we all want a
happy and successful career with a great paycheck
or you wouldn't be reading this book and trying to
plan for your military career. Consider into your
equation that each branch of service promotes at a
different pace.

In my nearly 12 years of service with the Army,
I've been able to see my friends in other services
get promoted and by that comparison with my
own career, I've been able to determine that the
Army has one of the faster promotion rates. Now,
with that being said, each career field within each

branch promotes at different speeds as well. Promotion rates are considered based on factors such as how long it takes for someone to move in or out (of the military), and up or down (in rank).

Consider this scenario: at one Walmart location, the store has 3 manager positions. The assistant managers with the most experience are all competing for positions as they come available. Once those leadership positions are filled, it's a waiting game until one manager relocates, gets promoted, demoted, or fired at which time, the position opens up for the next most qualified applicant. If on average, it takes a manager two years to qualify for the next position, you assume how long you may have to remain before you could potentially qualify for that position.

If we were to compare the same understanding to cashiers, we may find that cashiers promote faster to the next position because cashiers don't stick around to be cashiers for very long before they look for something more desirable.

Retention and Career Satisfaction

Retention is crucial for keeping the skilled and experienced troops in the service because it allows for a stronger and more capable military force. Failure to keep the highly qualified Soldiers will only weaken our country's ability to adapt and develop over time because our military will be forced to continue training brand new troops for service. Having long term experience within our military formations will give us the advantage of evolving our capabilities into the future.

Retention cannot be accomplished without career satisfaction. Let's face it, if you're doing a job that you hate for an organization that you don't fully support, you're not going to hang around. You're going to always look for the greener grass, the better paycheck, the greater opportunities. However, if you enjoy your organization and believe in the mission, you're going to stick around even at the most challenging times. If you're being taken care of financially and you're satisfied with your opportunities, you're going to hang around and make a great career for yourself.

I encourage you to speak with those you know who have served in each branch and ask them questions regarding how long they served, what their overall experience was, how much time did it take for them to achieve their highest rank, etc. Take these answers into consideration so that you can see the bigger picture and decide which service is right for you.

Opportunities

Within each branch, there are unique opportunities. They can come in the form of special skill schools like parachutist school (airborne), sniper school, diver school, language training, job certification courses, etc. These unique schools are not universally offered among each branch and troops from some branches have a harder time getting access to certain schools over others. Some branches of the military have funding and availability to send troops to schools while other branches may struggle to enjoy that luxury.

Each branch has different mission requirements that offer more or less opportunities to attend schools. It is vital that you do your homework to see what unique schools are offered for the branch you're considering. Talk with those who have served in those branches to determine if certain schools are even feasible for your career but don't put a lot of weight into your decision of a branch because of this alone. These opportunities are nice because they give you extra skills and may help you compete for promotions but don't allow them to dictate your decision if they have no relevance to your long-term career plans. In the wise words of late Dr. Stephen R. Covey, "Begin with the end in mind."

Deployments

If you've never served in the military, the term "deployment" is probably the most frightening aspect of serving altogether. Images of war-torn countries and battlefields come to mind for most. Of course, not all deployments are bad. In fact, the term deployment is very broad.

Websters Dictionary defines deployments as: placement or arrangement (as of military personnel or equipment) in position for a particular use or purpose. Simply put, when troops are "deployed" it means they were sent to a location to use their skills to complete a mission. This could mean that Army medics from Fort Hood, Texas were deployed to Haiti to aid in an Ebola outbreak, or Navy diver's being deployed off the coast of Puerto Rico to search for aircraft wreckage.

As you can see, the term deployment doesn't necessarily mean being sent to war. With that understanding, deployments happen quite frequently, but it's nothing to be afraid of.

Deployments mean different things for different career fields and for different branches of service. Each branch has its area of focus. The Army is the mainland ground force, and the Navy patrols the seas. The Air Force governs the air, and the Marine Corps focuses on a combination of air, land, and sea. The Coast Guard maintains control of the U.S. coastline. So when a unit from any one of these branches is deployed, this helps you to understand where they may be geographically and what their mission will be focused around.

Benefits

You may hear recruiters talk a good game about how their branch can offer you benefits like free college education or the ability to buy a home with no money down because you served. Trust me, I've done my fair share of talking up the Army. The fact of the matter is most of the benefits you receive from any one of the branches is actually offered because of the Veterans Administration (VA).

These benefits are widespread and are not specific to one branch or another so no matter what branch you decide to serve with, you will receive these benefits. These benefits include but are not limited to the two versions of G.I. Bill (Montgomery and Post 9/11), the V.A. home loan, tuition assistance, and the twenty-year retirement pension. Do your research to see what benefits are currently being offered at the time you're considering enlisting.

YOUR RECRUITER IS

A SALESMAN

If you're between the ages of 17 and 24 and you have a heartbeat, you've probably received countless calls, texts, emails, social media, and face-to-face encounters with military recruiters. They are absolutely relentless at trying to persuade you to join their branch of service. Why? Because they're in the game of sales. They're trying to sell you on the idea that their product (military branch) is more superior than the competition. Just like a business, each branch wants to be the first to get your business. They want to close the deal with you before they get beaten by their competition. They become hungry, ruthless, and even annoying at times to ensure that they get to you first. It's their duty.

Keep in mind that while this is happening, it is also YOUR duty to check out what each service has to offer so you don't miss out on a better opportunity. Just as I stated in the previous chapter, each service is different. As such, each can help or hinder your ability to reach your goals if you're not focused on the end result. You cannot go into the service without keeping your end goal in mind. If you fail to keep your attention on your short and long term agenda, you'll lose sight in the day-to-day grind and ultimately settle for whatever comfort zone you have drifted into.

Your recruiter was once in your shoes

Believe it or not, your recruiter was once in the same dilemma as you are now; to join or not join the military. I can almost guarantee you, that when they enlisted they never thought they would be a salesman for their branch. They probably had visions of going to the range, riding in humvees, and training in the field. They probably spent many years in their job doing what they love doing but at some point in their career, they were hand-picked to work a job in recruiting for a few years. Now their job is no longer to lead and train their team; it's making cold calls to teenagers, visiting high schools, and trying to promote how awesome their branch of the military is. To some, this comes easy. Maybe they're naturally extroverted and enjoy the hunt for their next recruit. To others, this may be the most challenging thing they have done in their careers. However, to nearly all of them, this is not what they wanted to do in the service, so they're trying to make the most of it.

Recruiting is one of the necessary roles that allow the military to remain an all-volunteer service. It's a challenging assignment for most but offers the potential for faster promotion and individual recognition. Some recruiters volunteered for the challenge, while others are told to take the new position. Understand what your recruiter's situation maybe and I assure you that you will treat them far differently than just an annoying recruiter.

Not all recruiters are created equal

Walk into any recruiting office of any branch and you will see people from all walks of life, with different goals and aspirations. Throughout their careers with the military, each recruiter has chased their own personal dreams. By doing so, each has encountered completely different experiences in the service. Some recruiters may have traveled around the world multiple times and experienced new cultures. While others may have remained in the U.S. and worked in a variety of jobs.

With each new experience they have had comes one more talking point they share with you. So when you're talking with your recruiter, understand that the knowledge they share, most of the time is based on their personal experiences. Each recruiter is a wealth of unique experiences. But not every recruiter can answer the questions that you may be seeking because of their experiences or lack thereof. It's important to talk with others who may have had experience in dealing with whatever questions you are looking for answers to.

Your recruiter has a quota

That's right. Your recruiter has a quota. This is the number of contracts that he or she is required to produce on a month-to-month basis but you've probably already heard this, perhaps as a rumor. This is your recruiter's mission. The reason for this is to ensure that their military branch has the manpower to meet it's mission goals since each year people are leaving the service to chase new careers.

So what does this mean for you? First, it means that they will feel a certain pressure from their supervisors to get you through the process of joining in a very timely manner. In turn, they may put the pressure on you, so don't take it personally. If you're committed to joining their branch, they want to help you get it done as quickly as possible. However, if you're telling your recruiter that your going to join but are dragging your feet through the process, you may get endless phone calls, or even surprise visits at your house by your recruiter. It might feel like harassment, but I assure you, the recruiter doesn't want to harass you any more than you want to be harassed. Be open and honest with your recruiter. Let them understand your intentions upfront so they know how to approach working with you. It will make everyone's lives easier.

Your recruiter is just not that into you

Now that you understand the quota and the reason for it, you need to know that your recruiter is not going to give you much, if any, time out of their day if you're not qualified or committed to joining. Everyone loves window shopping when it comes to the military. It gives them a warm and fuzzy feeling about how awesome their life could be if they took action and joined. Sadly the case is that most will talk to a recruiter, or several recruiters, only to make themselves feel like they are doing something with their life. They won't however, commit to the decision. No recruiter has time for window shoppers because they have no intention to "buy." A recruiter's time is too precious to waste on people who will never make that decision. From a recruiting standpoint, they have to move on and talk to others who are willing to pull the trigger and commit to their future.

That's not everybody, of course. Some people would enlist at the drop of a dime but something else is holding them back; maybe obesity, or a medical issue. These are all very common problems as well. Even though you maybe 110% ready to enlist, your recruiter still can't do much to help you because of your current limitations. It's because of this that they cannot give you all the time you may need. Recruiting is a numbers game and he who has the most numbers wins.

If you're fortunate enough to not have any medical issues, law violations, weight problems, or commitment issues, then I can almost guarantee you that your recruiter will bend over backward to help you out. You're like an easy paycheck. They have to work more hours and jump through many more hoops for any of the problems previously mentioned and even then, there is no guarantee that you'll be able to join after it's all said and done.

It's strongly encouraged that if serving in the military is something you really want to do, do it when you're young. Every day that you get older is one more opportunity for a problem to creep into your life and potentially prevent you from serving your country.

Kevin W. Porter

THE ENLISTMENT PROCESS

Once you've decided to join the military and you've picked your branch, you're going to be jumping through hoops to get qualified. This process is a quick breeze for some and a long grueling nightmare for others. If you understand what is taking place behind the scenes, it may be easier for you to relax and be patient knowing that your recruiter is doing all they can for you.

Step 1: Meet with your recruiter

Before you plan to meet with a recruiter, there are a few things you need to understand about the recruiter's job. Every recruiter, regardless of branch, is responsible for determining if an applicant is qualified or disqualified for service. After determining that you're qualified, they will discuss what is possible for your career with their branch of service. After you have made the commitment to join, they will facilitate the process of helping you enlist. This means your recruiter does not enlist you. Well, not directly anyway. In fact, the process of enlisting doesn't actually take place within a recruiting office but instead at MEPS (Military Entrance Processing Station). Your recruiter helps build your application, collects necessary documents, and schedules your processing at MEPS.

I bring this up because a lot of people get cautious about meeting with recruiters at their office because they're afraid of signing a contract unknowingly. Parents are even more cautious but the truth is, it's just not the case. Recruiters do not have the authority to draft contracts on their level.

Once you've scheduled a time to meet with a recruiter, start collecting up all of your personal documents such as your birth certificate, social security card, passports, high school diploma, proof of paid traffic tickets, and any medical documents if you've ever been to the hospital for anything more serious than a common cold. By having these documents together from the get-go, you are helping your recruiter to determine your eligibility for serving. Most people overlook the simple fact that just because you have a heartbeat and a desire to serve your country that you are actually eligible to serve. Periodically, each branch of military changes its criteria for qualified recruits. The only way you will know for sure if you're making the cut is by having that conversation with your recruiter and bringing all of your supporting documents to the table.

When you're first talking with your recruiter and getting pumped up about the exciting adventure you're about to embark on, you need to be completely transparent about your past. Every little detail about your medical history needs to be disclosed because recruiters have to plan your physical screening with the MEPS doctors based on these details. When you're meeting with the doctors, they will ask you for all of this information as well so it's important to be upfront about everything in your medical history. This way, what your recruiter tells MEPS and what you tell the MEPS doctor are the same. Failure to get this right could potentially disqualify you from serving, depending on the severity of the medical issues. So don't leave it up to your memory to recollect your medical past. Gather your medical documents and provide them to your recruiter.

You also need to be forthcoming about any run-ins with the law as well. If you've ever been arrested, tell your recruiter. If you've ever been pulled over, tell your recruiter. If you've ever gotten a red light camera ticket, tell your recruiter. You get the idea. Regardless of what the charge was, or if your charges were dropped, sealed, or expunged, your recruiter needs to know about it. During your processing, you will be fingerprinted so that your recruiter can get your criminal record from the FBI. If you decide to keep secrets about your past, I assure you that your recruiter will find out. Once it comes to light that you were hiding something in your past, they will be less trusting of you and much less interested in helping you land a career with their branch.

Step 2: Take the ASVAB test

As we talked about earlier, the ASVAB is the exam you must complete in order to determine whether you have the intellect to serve. This test will be the determining factor in what jobs you qualify to serve in. Typically this test is conducted at MEPS and can take about three hours to complete. There are also paper versions of this test that can be administered in locations other than MEPS. High schools usually offer the

Student ASVAB (SASVAB) which allows students to complete the test without having to miss a day of school. Additionally, there is another form of the ASVAB known as the Pre-screening Internet-Delivered Computer Adaptive Test (PICAT) that allows military applicants to complete the exam in the comfort of their home without the strict time limit that comes with taking the standard ASVAB. In order to prevent cheating, participants of the PICAT must complete a verification exam at MEPS; which is a quick and condensed version of the PICAT to confirm there has been no cheating during the initial test.

Once you've completed the ASVAB testing, your recruiter will be able to discuss with you if you're intelligent enough to serve in the Armed Forces. Keep in mind that each branch has different standards as to what scores are considered to be passing. If you score too low to qualify with one branch, you may still be eligible to join a different branch. These minimum score standards are subject to change periodically based on the needs of the branch. If you do not qualify for any branch of the military, get back to the books and study so you can retake the ASVAB.

If you passed the ASVAB, it's at this point that
your recruiter can talk about the jobs you
currently qualify for. Keep in mind, as I had
discussed in chapter 4, that your job options may
be limited based on the availability of jobs within
that branch. The recruiter may not be able to offer
you a guaranteed job, but rather a specific field of
interest. Job availability comes and goes based on
what the branch is hiring for at the given moment.
So while you may be qualified for your dream job
today, if it still takes you 4 more weeks to finish
the process of enlisting, that job is likely to be
gone.

Step 3: The physical screening

If you've made it this far, congrats! The ASVAB
filters out a large percentage of applicants. With
that being said, the physical screening filters out
an even larger percentage of applicants.

If you've brought any medical issues to your
recruiter's attention, it is at this point that they are
waiting for approval from the Chief Medical
Officer (CMO) to give you the approval to go to
your physical examination at MEPS. This can
take some time depending on how many medical
records the doctor has to review, so be patient.

Once the CMO has reviewed your file, they may say you're cleared to physical, or that you've been denied because your medical issues are too concerning and you may not be physically qualified for military service. If you're lucky enough to be approved, get ready for a long day at MEPS.

The physical screening will typically start around 6 a.m. and can last 6–8 hours depending on how many people are going through the physical with you. It's during this process that you will be examined for vision and hearing. You'll be doing different mobility movements like the duck walk. The doctors will look over your body for anything that stands out as unusual like scars or abnormal growths. If you had medical issues as I mentioned before, this is the point where the doctors will take a closer look at you to see if the issues are a problem. If you pass the physical, congrats. Now you have one more step in the process.

Step 4: Meet with the career counselor

You're in the home stretch. This is the last phase in the enlistment process that thins out the remaining qualified recruits. You have reached this point when you have passed the ASVAB and physical but now you have to discuss all your law violations, past financial problems and have your medical file reviewed so that all can be factored in to determine if you're eligible for the job you want. Rest assured that this point in the process is actually the least problematic for most recruits. Maybe you're not like most recruits. If you've been honest and forthcoming with your recruiter about your past problems, they should have set you up for success. If, after having the discussion with the guidance counselor, you've been given the green light to enlist, you will review your contract that will outline your years of service obligation, any incentives that you're receiving, and the job or field that you will be trained in during your first term. If you agree to the terms, sign the line and proceed to take the oath of enlistment. This oath is the first right of passage for all service members.

Step 5: Pre-Basic Training - Delayed Entry Program (DEP)

Now that you've enlisted, it's time to prepare for Basic Training. This time before you leave for training, you're considered a member of the Delayed Entry Program or DEP. Your recruiter is going to be working with you periodically to help you get into shape and ensure that you're not going to have any trouble shipping off to training. This time will be spent exercising and learning about the branch that you have joined. Take this training seriously because it can make life a lot easier for you when you get to boot camp.

If you've enlisted into the Reserve or National Guard, this point in the process will be a little different. The reason is once you've taken the oath of enlistment, you're officially in the Reserve or National Guard. You can begin attending "Drills." This is your one weekend a month duty with the military, working at the unit that you have been assigned to. Your recruiter should take you to your unit and get you familiar with the personnel that you'll be working with.

Since you're going to be working with your unit, you will also be given a military ID card so that you can get onto your base. Active-duty personnel will receive their military ID once they arrive at basic training. This ID card will validate that you work for the military and will give you access to government buildings and equipment as well.

Although you have not been officially trained, your time spent working at your unit on drill weekend will be to start learning the duties of being a service member. Your supervisor will help you get familiar with your job and how operations work around your unit. When you work on drill weekends you will receive payment for your work. Make sure you discuss with your recruiter and your unit when you should be expecting your first paycheck.

Step 6: Boot Camp

The day has arrived and it's time to ship off to training. Chances are, you won't sleep much the night prior and the first day or two of basic training. This is where everything starts getting real.

When you arrive at the base, you won't be going straight into basic training. Instead, you will first begin with in-processing at a "reception" unit. Reception is the first step of basic training and will usually last around four days. The sole purpose of reception is to get you officially checked in to the military. The experience is going to feel a lot like being on an assembly line because you will be sharing the moment with hundreds of other recruits. You will move through many different sections of in-processing, from medical where you will receive a variety of shots, to equipment and uniform fitting.

Reception can be the most unexciting aspect of basic training because it's your first initial shock of the military, but it is nothing like what you envisioned you'd be going through. Stay positive and remember that fun times are ahead.

Kevin W. Porter

THE ASVAB TEST

The ASVAB is the Armed Services Vocational Aptitude Battery test. If you haven't caught on yet, the military loves their acronyms. This test measures your knowledge and comprehension of four domains: math, verbal, science and technical, and spatial. Each of these components are broken down into the following subcategories:

General Science - Knowledge of physical and biological sciences.

Arithmetic Reasoning - Ability to solve arithmetic word problems.

Paragraph Comprehension - Ability to obtain information from written passages.

Word Knowledge - Ability to select the correct meaning of a word presented in context and to identify the best synonym for a given word.

Mathematics Knowledge- Knowledge of mathematic principles at the high school level.

Auto and Shop Information - Knowledge of automobile technology and of tools and shop terminology and practices.

Electronics Information - Knowledge of electricity and electronics.

Mechanical Information - Knowledge of mechanical and physical principles.

Assembling Objects - Ability to determine how an object will look when it's parts are put together.

Your understanding of the first four subjects will be vital if you want to qualify for serving in the military, but it is the combination of all of these subjects that will impact your eligibility for any particular career field. Each branch has minimum scores required to qualify for certain jobs. Some jobs may even require multiple minimum scores to qualify. Very specialized jobs may require, in addition to the minimum scores, that you have certain high school or college classes completed. This is why it is important to plan ahead at an early age so you can set yourself up for success. Those who do not plan ahead, but rather rely on the military as a backup plan, often find themselves with a lack of options when they finally decide to serve.

The Armed Forces Qualifying Test (AFQT) score is the number most commonly referred to as the ASVAB score. This score determines whether you passed the exam and whether you scored high enough to join the branch you want. Your score can range between 1 and 99. The ASVAB is not graded on a percentage basis as most traditional tests are. Instead, the ASVAB is graded on a percentile basis. A national study conducted in 1997 among students between 18 and 23 completed this test. Based on the results, it was determined that approximately half of the students scored above 50 on the exam. What can be deducted from this information is that if you score a 65 on the ASVAB, the score suggests that you scored as well as or better than 65% of the students who tested for the study in 1997.

When you begin working with a recruiter, you're likely to take a practice ASVAB test that will indicate your strengths and weaknesses of the complete ASVAB. There are a variety of practice tests available online as well. Take advantage of the free resources available online that can help you prepare for the ASVAB. It's important that you study and practice ahead of time so that you score your best because just passing the ASVAB is not enough. Some branches of the military only allow you to take the ASVAB until you have a passing score. If you take the ASVAB and score a 40, that maybe the score you are stuck with. Unfortunately, if you fail the ASVAB, you may be required to wait for 1 month, all the way up to 6 months before you can retest. If for some reason you're not satisfied with your AFQT score, you may be able to retest once you've enlisted and have completed your initial training.

Why does retesting matter once you've enlisted? Depending on the branch you join, you may be able to retrain into a new job at various points throughout your career. This will depend on the branch you serve in. Be sure to ask your recruiter about the feasibility of changing jobs.

HOW TO MAKE THE

MOST OF YOUR

CAREER

As I have mentioned several times throughout this book, it is crucial that you begin your career with the end in mind. It's never wise to begin a job, only to realize half-way through it that you were never going to reach your end-state. You wouldn't start washing a load of clothes if you knew that you couldn't dry them. The same holds true that you shouldn't start working in one career field if you know that it doesn't align with the long-term plan for your life. It's not enough to join the military and just work for a paycheck. First, there is no fulfillment in that task alone. Secondly, someday you're going to leave the military, and if you haven't planned your career for what comes next, you will be hard-pressed to find a civilian employer who will take you in.

Employers love hiring Veterans. They make great leaders in the workplace with their strong work ethic, and quick decision-making skills. It's a no brainer but let's be realistic. If you don't possess the skills or qualifications required for the job, you're not going to be their first choice. The military is willing to pay you as they train you. It's not so advantageous for an employer to do the same.

This chapter is going to help you plan the necessary steps to ensure that you start your career on the right foot. As you get a little experience under your belt, ensure you find a mentor who has walked the path you are pursuing so that you have more one-on-one guidance for all the questions you might be asking.

Hopefully, if you've gotten to this point, you've considered the types of jobs you would be most interested in. Keep in mind, that you may not qualify for certain jobs for any number of reasons. For instance, you are considering military police as a viable job because you would like to gain the experience of being a Cop. However, the Army may not authorize you to take that job if you have negative drug or alcohol history or significant problems with your driving record.

As you begin talking with your recruiter, they will help you understand what challenges you may face and plan accordingly. As I've said before, your recruiter is not a miracle worker and is primarily concerned with helping you enlist. You may not possess the skills or education to justify getting a job you're asking for so have an open mind throughout the process.

1. Study for and take the ASVAB

I cannot stress the importance of studying for this test. As I mentioned in the previous chapter, understanding and preparing for the ASVAB is vital to creating your opportunities. When you begin working with a recruiter, you will be able to take a practice test. This will help gauge your knowledge of the subjects that will determine your eligibility to serve. The subjects not covered in the practice test will determine your career options.

When I say study for the ASVAB, I'm implying that you actually put deliberate effort into learning about the subjects that are being covered. The test is focused on high school level subjects. If you weren't paying attention during school, then just studying isn't going to help. You'll need a tutor to help break things down in a fashion you can understand. Studying alone is best suited for those who need to refresh their memory on what they've learned. If you know you need the extra help, find it. Don't waste time trying to figure things out for yourself. You'll find yourself just spinning your wheels and getting nowhere.

2. Use the ASVAB Career Exploration Program

The asvabprogram.com website has many great resources to help determine which career field is most suited for you based on your test scores. This site will also survey your interests and help you to identify potential careers that align with your strengths. It may help open your mind to more possibilities you may not have previously considered.

3. Select a career that is related to your long-term studies.

If you prepare for the ASVAB, you should do well. That will impact your ability to land a career in a job or field that you desire as long as the branch you're pursuing actually offers that career. It is wise for you to discuss with your recruiter what opportunities will be available for you throughout your military career. Each job will offer special training and chances to expand on your knowledge of your career. If you demonstrate the potential to take on leadership responsibilities, you will be able to attend advanced training within your field. This will further your career opportunities and improve your resume.

4. Use the Joint Service Transcript for college credits

The Joint Service Transcript is much like any college transcript in the sense that it keeps a record of all of your completed military education. During your time in the military, you will continue to add new education and courses to your transcript. When you start planning your college education, submit your Joint Service Transcript to your college so they can evaluate your military education and give you college credits. If your career in the military is relatable to what you're studying in school, it's likely that you will get credits toward your degree. That means you can complete your education in a shorter period of time. It also means that it will reduce the financial burden that your education can have on you. Working on and completing your college education can also help you qualify for more competitive promotions while you're serving.

5. Volunteer

One of the quickest ways to develop in a career field with little or no skills is to volunteer. Most people think of volunteering like helping out within the local community by cleaning up the streets, working at an animal shelter, or cooking meals for the homeless but that isn't always the case. What I mean by volunteering is to step up into positions of greater responsibility so that you can be trained and mentored. This kind of professional development is sought after by top performers, the go-getters. These self-motivated individuals are often those who excel through the ranks at a much faster rate than that of their peers. It's because the military is seeking those who are driven to do more and perform their best.

In the Army, we have career "maps." These "maps" help Soldiers to identify potential assignments and positions within their job that will further develop them in their skillset. By having these "map," individuals can see exactly what opportunities lie ahead in their careers and plan accordingly. Without a map, you might find yourself getting lost on your journey. This is no different from having a goal without a plan. The intent is to give you clear steps you must take to expedite your development. By doing so, you will advance through your career much faster.

Kevin W. Porter

TAKE A LEAP OF

FAITH

I hope this book has helped to provide you with some direction and points of consideration for your military career. I offer this advice because I feel strongly about taking care of those who decide to make serving their country a personal responsibility. Not everyone can join the military. For the few that can and do serve, it is our responsibility to ensure they are guided with genuine care. It is my personal belief that if you've been taken care of up-front with your decision to serve and provided the best information to make a decision, you will be a better Soldier. Additionally, you will have the wisdom and responsibility to pass on guidance to others.

One of the greatest traits of the military is how helpful each service member is to one another. Everyone wants to succeed and see others succeed as well. It's what makes the U.S. military the greatest military in the world.

Of course, taking the leap of faith is easier said than done. Many who consider joining the military often talk themselves out of making the decision. Some will try to weigh the pros and cons of their decision until they have lost interest in the pursuit altogether. This is referred to as analysis paralysis. This alone can waste so much of your time and kill many of your dreams. It's your internal self-doubt that is talking to you. What your doubts do not know is the great opportunities that wait for you on the other side of your fears. Do not dwell on the doubts, the fears, and the unknowns. A year from now you can look back and say to yourself "I wish I had joined already" or "I'm glad I joined already." It takes action to get the results you desire. If you find that your current situation is not producing those results, then maybe you need a serious change in your course. Don't hold yourself back from making positive changes in your career because you don't have all the answers you need to make a decision. Nobody has all the answers. Take action and adjust your course along the way.

Now you have a decision to make. Join the U.S. Military and protect our great nation, or continue on your current path. For me, it was a no-brainer. The decision to serve has been the proudest accomplishment of my life, as it has been for many others.

Each person has a path to follow, and yours may or may not be military service. If you have been giving the thought of joining some serious consideration, it may be because your current path is not satisfying your ambitions. Perhaps serving may be the helping hand you need to get your life on track as it was for me. It will take an enormous amount of courage on your part to make the decision, but consider the person you will become in the process.

When I look back on who I was to who I became, there is a substantial difference. I contribute the positive change in my life to how the Army has pushed me beyond my personal boundaries. I found myself outside of my comfort zone more often than not. As I learned how to find comfort in exceeding my limitations, I started pushing my ambitions higher and higher.

If you feel as though you are not living up to your fullest potential, I encourage you to serve. Take the opportunity and grow from it. You will find more confidence and ambition on the other side.

ABOUT THE AUTHOR

Kevin Porter started his career with the Army in 2008. During his service, he worked in many states along the East coast and completed two deployments in the middle east. He worked as a Geospatial Engineer with the Special Operations Command in Fort Bragg, NC and as a Recruiter with the Recruiting Operations Command in Long Island, NY.

In 2019, Kevin honorably separated from the Army to pursue new opportunities in his business, investing, and writing career.

Kevin is originally from Lexington, North Carolina. When he's not overly caffeinated and working his commerce company, he's usually outside hiking, kayaking, or mountain biking.

You can find Kevin on most social media channels @kevinwporter.

Made in the USA
Monee, IL
14 March 2023